The Scatter and the Gap

The Scatter and the Gap

Poems

Patricia Horn O'Brien

GRAYSON BOOKS
West Hartford, Connecticut
graysonbooks.com

The Scatter and the Gap
Copyright © 2023 by Patricia O'Brien
Published by Grayson Books
West Hartford, Connecticut
ISBN: 979-8-9855442-3-7
Library of Congress Control Number: 2022918892

Interior & Cover Design by Cindy Stewart
Cover Image: "All in Pieces" by Judy Perry

Contents

So, Here's the Scatter and the Gap 9

AT LARGE

Deus ex Machina 13
And Almost Home 14
Who Learns 15
How to Seed a Pomegranate 16
A Dozen, 17
Ant on a Rock 18
Brief Summer 19
What the Road Portends 20
Calling Hours 22
Michael, we all left 23
Transformation 25
Getting Somewhere 26
Mercy Center Prayer Basket Reconsidered 27
Princess of the Sand 29
Fish Kill 30
Studying Wildlife from I-95 31
Preparations for a Visit 32
About Time 33
Beyond What You Know 34
Who Dies 35
Disconnected 36
Getting to Prayer 37
Grief's Parapet 39
Something's Lost 40
Quest 41
Lockdown 42
Nose Job or Contemplating the Relative World 43

Whose Question   44

Jackie   45

Higgs Boson Leads the Way Back to Empty Space and
    All That It Contains   46

In Birmingham, Once Upon a Time, Circa 1940   48

Watch Out   49

When Buttons for Sale Were Sewn onto Paper Strips
    and We Walked to Work and Time Flew   50

2160 E. Tremont Avenue, The Bronx   51

Good Enough   52

What It Takes   54

WORKADAY

How the Bus Driver Took Us for a Ride   57

For M., Visiting Nurse   58

The Social Worker Rehearses What She'll Say   59

Regarding Grief's Particulars   60

Although I Am the One Sent to Help   61

Visiting Nurses, Bridgeport, Connecticut, circa 1985   62

The Social Worker Takes Note   63

A Lesson in Listening   64

STARTING OUT

How She Escapes   66

So Soon   69

Grief's Job   70

I've Tried to Say This Before   71

Children's Hour   72

In a New York Minute   73

In the End   74

Pushing "M" for Main   75

Hope's Design   76

Choosing the First Among Equals   78
Linen takes the hottest iron,   80
My Mother Thought to Watch Out for Me   81
The Gathering   85
Letter from a Day at the Beach Bereft, July 9th   86
Surrender Is at Least as Sweet   87
The Earth   88
Taking Care of Birds and Other Small Creatures   89
The Buddhists Say   91
Grappling   92

AND SO
Revisiting a Youthful Conversation on Love's Meaning   95
Cold in the Country, Notwithstanding   97
Reverie   99
This fly,   100
Without a Word   101
For the Girl Who'd Make Poems of Whales   102
Grief: A Tip or Two on How to Handle It   103
Joy and How to End It   104
Not that Far   105
A Lesson in Alternative Medicine   106
Summer's Prosody   107
By Happenstance: A Tale   108
Losing Sight   110
Lull   111
You Question the Recommendation   112
Knowing Almost Everything   113

Notes   114
About the Author   116
Acknowledgments   117

So, Here's the Scatter and the Gap

In response to Judy Perry's painting *All in Pieces*

The scatter that wakes you from the trance
that made you think you had it right, that
you were in charge, that life is as certain
as the toast you are going to make when you get
out of bed. As certain as your plan to call your friend.
Certain as the front door. The key in your hand.

Then comes the cracking up. The break apart
that tears you from your certain breakfast.
That takes your friend. That blasts your door
off its hinges and leaves you with the useless
key you fling across the grass.

Maybe it's then it begins. You let yourself
collapse before the altar of this mess. You
take a breath. You say, *Of course!* You say,
Oh, yes. And in a day or week or slew of weeks
you stand up in the gap that arrives when you
abandon all you thought you knew and open
to whatever happens next.

At Large

Deus ex Machina

This night's steely rain obliterates
the highway's white dashes and dots
and in the soaked dark you veer
onto the bright red tracks the 18-wheeler

sets down straight ahead in your distress,
even as the scattered beacons of, say,
a house, a gas station, a parking lot,
fly past with useless traces you can't

add up in your mirror amok
with clinging rain and, out loud, you bless
the trucker ahead, not to say pray, he'll
stay this race and neither sleep nor skid nor slip

away, but steer you
on the slick,
steadfast tracks of his largess.

And Almost Home

He'd only just added
three French phrases,
one algebraic formula, ease

with his locker key.
He'd elbowed
his buddy in the hall.

Daydreamed

the night into being,
his favorite
Hey, cute thing!

just before maple leaves
garlanded the spikes
of his perfect hair, his sweet

smart-ass smile no guard
against the descent
of the undermined tree,

the wind with its last lesson.

Who Learns

Even while we chat and drink,
her father chops and sets out the salad
he's gathered from this year's
reticent garden. Each bowl

displays the pretty touch of red he's
centered there. His knives
gleam.

Her mother's still gaze beseeches us
when we fail to speak.

From her perch on the dining room floor,
their daughter who neither speaks nor walks, jabs
our high air, her fallen bird call

puncturing our attempt at dinner talk.
This autumn she'll reach her majority.
Her father says she has taught them everything
for which they were not prepared.

How to Seed a Pomegranate

Fill a large bowl with cold water; then, slice the small crown off the top of the pomegranate. You should be left with something that looks like... —Sophisticated Gourmet

Memorize the earth's land and oceans.
And if you plan to swim, swim deep beneath
the surf but not below the fractured sun.
You will need to discover who you are
vis-à-vis volcanoes.
Wear a bib.

Prepare to delve. Look up
from the sink frequently to gaze across
the tidal marsh your kitchen window
frames with equanimity. While you probe,
probe like a surgeon barred from seeing
past her patient's skin and bone

but who peers far across the examining room,
testing what her fingers meet with what she's always known.

A Dozen,

        at least, discrete blackbirds
fly into the marsh behind our house,
a fluttering of daylight and dark,
an excitement in the August still,

welcome but so brief you blink but
once and not one bird remains.
Embraced so absolutely by the willowy grass
they no longer even seem. Once here,

now there, somewhere beyond all
we know of birds and grass. The marsh,
so perfect in its complicity, not
one ripple, not one broken blade...

providing, despite our logical insistence,
a dozen birds their essential non-existence.

Ant on a Rock

This is what you should have known: this ant
on this rock is this ant and this ant is this ocean
and this boat and this fish and this child and this moon
and this sunrise and this getting old and this coming

and going and this birth and this dying. This ant hauls joy
and sorrow. This ant knows what it is to climb and what
it is to miss a step. This ant knows what it is to stall and what
it is to go. This ant knows what it is to be undone

and neither chooses to stop nor to go, but simply stops
or goes. Here is the child within your ancient self. Here
escapes your *Oh, no!* Another day begins, another day
ends. *Oh, no!* And then again, *Oh, yes,*

here with the ant on the rock, with the going ahead,
with the dropping back. With the stopping right here, smack dead.

Brief Summer

circa 1949

Not much more than a shack
among rows of shacks, it rises

out of Long Beach sand, spiny
twitch grass and interlocking

gravel paths. The ocean's
somnolent measure of summer

lengthens its hours, the hours
passing, nonetheless. Does Mrs. Doyle,

my mother's country mouse friend,
know the earth's steady speed

is relentless? She folds line-dried sheets
onto the kitchen chair and instructs me,

her guest, to sit on its rising
white stack, my sandy feet lifting

off the linoleum floor. *Ironing,*
Mrs. Doyle calls it. And when,

dinner's last dish done, our breaths mingle
with the lift of the crackling sheets

we sail across our waiting beds,
summer's swift advance

that moment,
held.

What the Road Portends

1943 – 1951

Summer after summer
it's the same dust-covered trunk
filled with camp's end…the lake's grit sifted
among what gear's left after eight weeks'
sleepover at Little Flower Camp.

From my trunk's perch I watch
the road's dust rising up.
Rising up. Rising up. Each
cloud of car-lifted dust the only break
in the late summer's reckless haze.

Each car it delivers the only break
on the road's still stretch. Look up!
Or rather, I look up, look up
look up, into the lifted dust. Into the car
it delivers. I am the daughter.

Are you the father?
The mother? But out they come.
Not mine. Almost, but not.
I must reconsider.
Consider the time gone by.

Their certain look I left them with
at summer's bright start. Their height.
Their weight. The way my father's fedora
shaded his face. The way my mother
disappeared in his shade.

Into the sun they emerge. Not them. I look up
again. Again. Again. Not them. Until
the sun's long rays drag the trees' shade across
the road, I wait. On the mountain's crest
the sun hesitates.

Calling Hours

Brian was your cousin's son. In fact, your husband's
cousin's son. It's only now you know him at all,
snapshot-after-snapshot tacked up along
the sure route of his mourners' shuffle and stop

through Yalesville Funeral Home, 4 to 8 p.m.,
his less than half a life summed up all afternoon
with tributes to just how brave he'd been.
How he'd played golf just the day before he

succumbed to a heart that chemotherapy had overrun.
All 18 holes, his mother says again. His open casket
sports a mug for beer and golf balls for another
18 holes, wily props to foil the underworld. But what

trickster scattered these freckles across his cheeks?
Left his long-lashed lids without another blink.

Michael, we all left

For Mike (1942-1979)

       dutiful to the man
in shiny black who escorted us
from the embarrassed earth,
its steam-shoveled dirt
politely piled under a tarp.
Or a flag. I can't

remember which. Driving home,
I wondered if we had enough
beer to keep your mourning friends
content. And how you went down
that hole's damp, rough walls,
hidden but guessed.

Solemn moment, that last push
against the air. The November light.

The diggers must have blessed themselves
then heaved your early death
with sighs and muted grunts until
they felt the earth take charge.

But it was almost noon.

Union members break for lunch.
Did they pinch your flowers
for their lapels, your wooden box
their feasting table until 1 o'clock
accused them? Before they left,

did they shove you over your last

precipice, then spit and scratch
themselves?

I should have stayed to spy
on such dereliction.

Although it really doesn't matter. You
were where you were, nonetheless,
when we headed home with beer
and sandwiches.

Transformation

after John Copelin's painting Global Warming

Enter here and wait no more than it takes to become
smoke and fire. No more than it takes to lose all desire
for the sky's wide reach, its endless tolerance and light,
its geese, its clouds that flit or, finally, tiring and too grand,

drop the rain your backyard garden had in mind.
No more than it takes to forget the hills beyond your town,
rising pink with spring and innocent. At least you used to think
along those lines, of seasons' overnight arrivals, their stealthy

departures despite your wish for one more morning of daffodils,
of green, of wheat, of snow muffling the bent edges of your street.
But here, beneath this black horizon of no rising moon,
no setting sun, you insinuate yourself around the towers

you climb and climb, your fire burning down
what you once knew of winter, spring, summer, autumn.

Getting Somewhere

Despite the train's lurching advance, across the aisle
a young woman, worn down despite what you guess
must be her recent starting out, hauls from a plastic bag
meant for a lawn full of scattered leaves, a needle,

a thread, and the dismantled stuff left of a child's
battle with winter to begin her determined repair.
Chasing its bewildered batting before the hard line
of her advance, she snags the garment's gnarled,

undone seams. Tames first one escaping
sleeve. Then the next. And although she gives
no sign that you're invited into the circle
of her industry, stitch after foolhardy stitch

you are drawn to her industry. Stitch-
by-stitch, she takes you to *Yes*.

Mercy Center Prayer Basket Reconsidered

For Richard Tietjen

Although I've written *For Richard,*
I hold my note tentatively above the prayer basket
at the feet of the Virgin Mary until I add
In the hope you'll accept my good intention
in lieu of faith and make him better.

Neither Richard nor I believe
in the efficacy of prayer. We may,
I hope though, be in the right company
amidst the crooked wings
of these imprecisely folded squares.

I blow the still air above
their complicated edges and uncover
an invocation or two until I discover
that my fingers are fluttering
into this basket of companionable prayers.

Get well. Be well.
Stay well. Be safe.
Be sober. Wake up.
Live.

The basket nests
these scraps
touching here.
Touching there.

Speedy recovery
from breast cancer, please.
Quick release from his life, a wreck.

Healthy delivery of a sweetest pea.

A Sarah and a Peg pray together
on one open, spare sheet
For our best buddy's last days,
under which I finally tuck
my own, inexact prayer.

Princess of the Sand

"Saudi Princess...found guilty of adultery at age 19...publicly
executed alongside her lover." —*Washington Post*

With hips precisely honed by the legacy
of balancing children of her tribe,
firewood, and grain, she sideswipes
the hour the king proclaimed

was her bequest. Unencumbered
now by outside weight, full stride
she rushes to the sea where she
will dance unveiled to drown

and rise again to die before her father
and his men. We of slender bones alike
who gather clues along the beach,
who tremble at the touch of sand,

foresee this legacy rewound,
cry out against her death, our own.

Fish Kill

This mid-December late afternoon
is being bullied toward tomorrow
  by a fractious squall undermining the day's
  predestined end
    at 4:42 p.m.

        Gulls,
wild as the shuttle they ride,
    precision dive onto a sprawled settlement
of beached fish, their shadows elongating
         toward night.

    Eyes gone. Bellies. Fins. That is,
if these fish ever had fins.
    Blind, they stare into the wind's
         indifference.

The fish.
    The gulls.
         And I,
    caught in some purposeful unknowing,
proffer my unwrapped face.
    My ungloved hands. The sand
tattooing all I offer to the wind.

    The gulls, now and then, glide back
aboard their wind's conveyance,
    waiting for something.

      The fish
lie still. Past afternoon. Past my *Goodnight!*
         Goodnight.

Studying Wildlife from I-95

The hawk snags a ride on high air,
a passenger so content, who of us
below thinks to factor in the pang
that will drive him through the day's

flat light into the trees' canopy?
And although we barely know
the catalog of wildlife's claw and beak,
its pragmatic give and take,

we imagine the field mouse, dumb
to his own significance, spying the hawk's
shadow devouring his path, his momentary
head, his tail, while all that's left

to us who watch from here,
the hawk's rise, his satisfied air.

Preparations for a Visit

For Florence.

As I wrap it for giving, this brass teapot
seems to have lost its weight, its ability
to carry meaning to the dying woman
I'm about to visit. The teas seem more

appropriate, herbs packed in one-ounce tins,
each with its answer to the questions of her body,
peppermint leaves and hibiscus for the lady
whose breasts and hair are gone. The teapot

will be for steeping. For warming her hands.
She is waiting for me. Still, I stall before my mirror.
Add a second touch of rouge to my cheeks.
In my own reflection I anticipate her eyes,

how they will grope for light. I'll recite, I decide,
How well you look! the teapot between us, a shield.

About Time

The six of us tromp the Vermont woods,
recent snow giving us the hold
we might otherwise lose

on this icy trail, an occasional slip
reminder of another danger the sun
half illuminates this gray afternoon.

Yes, the danger may be the ice,
but even as each of us plants one foot
before the next, the sun's pale path

shadows our uneasiness
with its strict measure of the six lives
this hour grants. But as we plow

our way back home, push aside one
and then another branch, cross the brook
in our longest boot-weighted strides,

we shake time loose. We laugh.
     New snow
         descends.

Beyond What You Know

after Judy Perry's painting Endless

Just at that spot the road
disappears from sight,
just where the river, once broad,

narrows and loses its light
to the reeds and wavering wall
of grassy might,

you stop, surprised by all
the aching clamor in your chest,
by tears rising to the pall

of mysteries beyond a crest
or stand of trees or sudden drop
on the path you'd kept from sadness.

Or so you'd tried. And without
a map to assure you what's just
out of sight, you know, on the spot,

sorrow's coming next...
But wait! You remind yourself.
Joy too will be waiting, quietly amidst

that absent scene, countervailing
weight against life's uncharted pain.

Who Dies

in response to Marie Howe's "The Last Time"

It's best mixed up: the you and I and
who is going to die, as if by twisting it

you drop down from the danger of it,
onto the bottom of a woods, say, all

roots and mossy shade or fly above
the atmosphere you've noted often,

so freighted with…not to overstate it…
pain or if not *nailed* pain, then

the risk of it. So, you, dear chap,
dear friend, dear passerby, dear aunt,

dear husband, dear girl on the bus
on the aisle in the hat…that's it,

the plaid hat with ear flaps against
the city's icy blocks, a power bar

in your backpack, a smart phone,
a date in your calendar you will

never make, your friend on the corner
you assigned, clutching his arms for heat,

wondering why you are late. Why you
haven't called. While you wonder why

all aboard this bus ignore the buzzer
someone pushed, the door springing wide.

Disconnected

after Peter Halley's painting Rectangular Prison with
Smokestack, 1987

The man-high wheel
of withered roots
and sodden earth,
unequal match
for this winter's
wind and ice,
looms larger now
than the felled tree's
heft and once majestic height
even as

the man
in his solitary cell,
hunkered over
his TV, dismantles
and ingests
dial / wire /
staple / screw
then waits
for the guard who'll try
to stand him up...to walk him...

somewhere.

Getting to Prayer

I'd given up saying Grace since it'd become clear
God had left the room of this universe. With no one
and nothing to thank but my own industry, my decision
to pull up my chair, I sank back and forked food without thought.

That was my phase of existential angst and it didn't last.
Now it suits me more to think of the path
my supper took, backward from the field greens on
my stoneware plate, to the refrigerator Shoreline Appliance

sold and delivered, the driver's neck wrapped in a paisley
do-rag, his back drenched, nevertheless. The drink
I offered, although barely cold enough for a man
hauling refrigerators. Next, to the market at Stop & Shop,

the crooked young man with a crooked spine (and other-
wise perfectly fine) sweeping corn silk and tracked-in sand…
   It's summer and somewhere there's a beach
     Somewhere an ocean…

from around the feet of the produce man, who dismantles
his tower of lettuce in crackling plastic stacks from
cart-to-cold counter. I've heard him talk
with another aproned man stacking pineapples,

each one a tribute to an absent sun, about
the looming threat of a walk-out. They shrug and
never lose the rhythm of their work. You can tell me
I'm reading in too much. But then

there's the truck. An 18-wheeler with a cab big enough
for sleeping and maybe a girlfriend to overturn the loneliness

of the long haul's drone. It's here I am stymied. Who with
a stoneware dish upon a woven table cloth can

imagine the act of harvesting endless rows of delicate leaves
stretched across fields of rain and the bitter sun
on either side of rain that grows all that's green and batters
those who bend to pick an eternity of lettuce? Amen.

Grief's Parapet

"...Entered into Eternal Rest, Sunday, January 9, husband of..."

On her driveway, our neighbor's car sits
on its balanced four wheels and squared
with the garage's white, automatic door.
The house's front door sits securely inside

its sturdy frame: red door and white frame
perfectly aligned and sealed against
this winter's hard edge. The venetian blinds
of every window down, but on a slant that,

we liked to think, might take in
the afternoon sun. Or, in the east windows,
dawn's slow coming around. But today when
we drive by, looking for her looking out a window

with a raised, if tentative blind, we only find
the car. The red door. The blinds closed and down.

Something's Lost

after Scott Kahn's painting March Moon

Neither those who drifted up the stairs
nor those who dawdle in the rooms below

know their share of earth has slipped
from twilight's breath between

what had been this day and the promise
of the next, and over tea she reviews

figures in her head, he tents his face
beneath *The Daily News* and rests,

upstairs the boy pivots in the glare
of his room's light overhead to find his

missing phone, in the mirror the girl
searches past herself to scan what she

reassures herself is hers, while the moon
inches the sky alone, the leafless tree, its

sorry echo, stealing into what had been
their summer's walled retreat across

yesterday's garden of sunlight,
across tomorrow's lost moon. Its rings of night.

Quest

After so much rain, the trees droop
with their newly accrued weight,

an aching green of leaves
and weariness. She's not sure

why she knows the path ahead
dips before it rises again, as if

it were her body's map,
a rhythm of breath,

a seeing before she looks
ahead, only to forget

what it means to proceed
beneath such trees, to feel the ground

rise and drop beneath feet that,
without being willed, move ahead.

Lockdown

a day in the Covid pandemic

Despite my bamboo blind
clattering up, despite my elbow
seeking my fallen strap

to send it to my shoulder's
angled quest, despite my eyelids,
aflutter with my window's

close offer of a sparrow's
still curiosity, she and I stare
each other into the speck of this hour,

neither she nor I adding anything
but the slender tether we allow.
I, awake to how the sparrow

and I are in it
together. She, awake,
and without a word about it.

Nose Job or Contemplating the Relative World

When I decided to have the aquiline rise
of my nose pared down, I'd already acquired
a career, a husband, 3 sons and
a Graduate Degree in Endlessly Caring.

I should have known better. Besides, I saw
how thoughts of my nose, no less my nose,
intruded themselves into the Center
of the Universe. Balance tottered, oh so

precipitously, toward chaos and finally stasis,
everything fallen away but my Self. But I
was afraid: I had glimpsed *The Future*
of The Witch in which nose and chin

join in a conspiracy of toothless
assay. Still, I worried
my decision was short sighted. Nonsense,
my surgeon assured me, *All peoples,*

no sooner out of the poor house and the risk
of starvation, turn their attention to self-
aggrandizement. Discretionary monies,
no sooner in evidence, are spent

on small beautifications.
Not on others' salvation.

Whose Question

What about the flickering leaves,
tree after tree, their pale

nether sides exposed
by a wind's shifting course.

Turned like the palms-up
of a bewildered citizenry,

they share a fleeting uncertainty.
The sun argues otherwise,

burning its confidence
past the hand you raise to shade

your eyes. But you know
the upturned leaves signal a storm,

if not just now, days along,
somewhere just beyond the horizon

you had always imagined
you had the vision to find.

Jackie

after Jac Lahav's painting, Jackie O.

Shot dead, your man toppled
           in the rat-a-tat
that split the bright Texas air.
      Bright and, despite November,
not without warmth enough

for an open car. And not without
love enough to line the long road.
Although, in the end, without heart enough

to give him back to you as good
as new and—well—as sweet
despite his peccadilloes, despite
Marilyn's breathless serenade. Still,

you wiped away the red insult
of his last farewell, removed
the hat pins from your bright pill box.
Shook out your coif.

And despite your reluctant legs, you stood up.
And despite the force of history stopped
mid-clock, you stood up. And despite
the pale hollow of the loss

that's held you to this spot,
one day you'll walk from here.
Your color back. Your hat.
         Your sorrow, our sorrow, intact.

Higgs Boson Leads the Way Back to Empty Space and All That It Contains

Higgs Boson in the Higgs field
is the toilet of modern physics,
Dr. Glashow observes, where beauty

gets its raucous start, and from there
the forms that carry it: a star,
your crowning child, the blossom

of light just before the sun goes down,
the walk you take at the water's
cool edge, the inevitable dive

deep, deep where you discover
no sadness follows, the intermittent
sound of your boys diving

wave-after-wave of happiness,
although they could not stop to
name it, any more than the man

planning to move into the infinitesimal
space of a NYC micro-unit, the toilet
a stone's throw, or then again, a glance,

a blink, a dream away
from the entrance and / or exit.
Lucretius had already ascertained

the way to ease our fears of gods
too terrible. (Take the floods and
pestilence those eons B.C.)

was to postulate nature's causes must
operate our world without any dark
god to say *Yea* or *Nay*...

But to name which cause,
Lucretius thought, lay beyond
the range of our stumbling

progress, that is until this day
a thousand physicists with
their gothic accelerator found the form

(or so they say) they sought in all
that emptiness, and out spins the man
in his tiny place, from toilet

to kitchen to computer, his bed tucked
somewhere beneath his toaster while you
drift to sleep, deep, deep under water.

In Birmingham, Once Upon a Time, Circa 1940

My mother didn't have much longer to live, as it turned out, when
she told me the story over tea…or of an evening over something
cold…in any case, coincidentally, of the day she pushed my
stroller into the lobby of a hotel on a Birmingham street where
down the block she'd spied a mob of white men building steam.
Breathless. Noose hot.

Did she leave me there by the bellhop to step one step outside the
        lobby door
to watch from the block's safe measure, that deadly scene? To
nudge closer to see that young man's face? The noose? Oh, I don't
know how to know the mean confines of that day. The heat. The
noise. The self-righteousness.

Or whether she never knew more of that street's shame, sheltered
        in the lobby's
upholstered get-away. Lullabying me. Sipping tea. Sashaying my
stroller. I don't know if we were guilty or innocent that deadly
day. And, in either case, to what degree? But by the time I realized
how little of that sorry tale I knew, my mother was gone.

Lost, her story. Mine. Our story, on that street in Birmingham.
The story of those men, start to end.

Watch Out

White birds dot the horizon of the rain-
flattened marsh, separated as precisely
as increments on a clock. But before
you think to count how many hours
they mark or know just what white birds
they are that measure the horizon,
they've flown into the rain from which

they apparently dropped, that rain which
came and came, taunting the grass for hours,
day into night, until your memory before
the storm no longer knows who you were precisely
and there, at your window, you let the horizon
waver and you become the relentless rain
until, despite your dreaminess, birds,

white alarms in the gray rain, white birds,
still and arranged as none you'd seen before,
silent and stern and…but how?…which
rouse you with their tidy presence on precisely
measured marks along the doused horizon:
as many as a dozen bright white hours
to wake you from the persistence of rain

but, friends, in what brief a time did rain
drop you into drowsiness again, from which
you wake to find no trace
                    of precise, white birds.

When Buttons for Sale Were Sewn onto Paper Strips and We Walked to Work and Time Flew

New York City, circa 1960

Leaves flew. Snow. Rain changed
the street to an angry stream.
Or sad. Our boots pressed us on.
Our soggy shoes.
Come on. Come on!
And on we went,
past

the basement window beside our flying feet,
grimy with every season of our flying by,
that grabbed our fleeting glance to frame
for those of us who deigned to look, the woman
bent over the reckoning of paper strips upon which

she sewed buttons she'd culled
and polished, culled and
polished, culled and
polished

while all the while leaves flew. The snow.
The rain rained. Sun came.
Leaves flew.

2160 E. Tremont Avenue, The Bronx

No window, no false door, no doorman;
no steep hill, no radio, no snap on, no
whistle, no cigar, no long list, no swing
set, no push cart, no *Hey you!*, no late
night, no nightlight, no shadow, no
entry, no escape, no desire, no today,
no lost thing, no old fool, no bra hook,
no take out, no A.C., no sidebar, no
highball, no trimmed hedge, no high
mark, no small crack, no pulled shade,
no sun rise, no cockroach, no brown
bag, no homework, no bride's dress, no
embrace, no landlord, no last cent, no
first thing, no trial run, no orange peel,
no pulled hair, no clothes line, no curb
ball, no staircase, no dropped note,
no latch key, no regret, no voice mail,
no pink slip, no MD, no quick left,
no mistake, no dove perch, no rough
night, no wet mop, no clock set, no love
nest, no time lost, no strange face, no
repair, no Greek god, no side-kick, no
saved day, no textbook, no brain scan,

no ring tone,
               no ride home,
no blind mice,
               no no thing.

Good Enough

Let us,
you and I,
eat this day,

its frost,
its bite,
its bitterness
its sweet after-
taste,

its sun's slash
across
the sea's fish-
drowning
deep,

its gulls
aloft in
unsettled shadows,
unsettled
breeze,

its visitors' tracks
above high tide's
watermark...
sneakers,
boots,

cleats, paws,
the echo
of their winter walk,
our walk.

We have the
teeth for it
and appetite.

What It Takes

In tribute to Mike Feder

On Saturday mornings, on WBAI,
Mike Feder fussed about his mother's
unpredictability and his own grown-up
miseries until, after enough Saturdays,

you knew your craziness was funny too.
When Mike Feder opined that
just getting out of bed was the bravest act,
you finally saw how brave you'd been

for years.   But that was then.   Now,
light strains to shine past the sleep mask
you wear to shut out the night street.
The dawn.

A worn-down resting place,
your mattress saps you of the will
wild enough to roll you
toward the bed's distant edge.

Until you remember how
Mike Feder's remedy for tragedy
and misfired therapy had cajoled you
into seeing the joke life is, and you

give up willing anything. You let
your body rise on the strength
of its own stored memory of what
it is to land your feet on the tufted rug.

What it is to disregard life's lack.
What it is to take a step.

Workaday

How the Bus Driver Took Us for a Ride

We'd thought somehow he'd make it. Just as he
must have made those sharp city turns, widening
the arc from the white line of his lane, his body
embracing the wheel, driving the angular beast

against its own momentum, so smooth the shifts
from south to east, north to west, so constant his cajoling,
any fear with which his riders came aboard lost its grip
even as they careened pole-to-pole. To us, he never

mentioned fear of death. Not even that he missed his old,
familiar route through Bridgeport's cratered streets.
He pulled one over on us, though, always asking how
we were doing. Always ready for a joke.

And we, his happy Hospice Team, lost track of just
where he was bound and just where he was taking us.

For M., Visiting Nurse

M: 1962-1990

She erased deadly words from her vocabulary. Minus words, she
said. Words, she said, that dragged her underneath the placid
surface of *All's well*. Beneath her just fineness. Or toward some
middle distance where lounge chairs settled. Where one's phone
line at work was disconnected. Access lost to electronic records.
Gone, the patients who needed her smart self,

her smile, regardless. Her blood pressure cuff, her referral to
Essential Services. She never put her feet up between home visits.
Between chemotherapy. Radiation. Between her son begging for a
ride to baseball practice. For peanut butter and jelly. Between the
late day glass of wine with her darling

who worries. Between naps and nausea, she constructed hardiness
phrases. Of the life that stays connected. She did all that until she
couldn't. Her phone went quiet. With a friend's mother, her son
got to his practice. Her husband sipped the day into evening by
himself. We can't say what failed her. We guess her happy words.

Her timecard sitting in Personnel. Her patients, waiting for their
next nurse. Her desk cleared and dusted.

The Social Worker Rehearses What She'll Say

If you begin with vague complaints about
your feet or how, since you've been left to fend
for yourself, it's been so hard to sleep without
disturbing dreams... Or if we spend
each minute rolling to the next, your voice
stringing this hour with little stones
of hard luck and lack of a decent place
to lay your head.   So weary.   So by yourself...

And if I steal little readings from the clock
too high upon the wall for an easy steal, will you
seek me in the distance of my furtive glance
and snap me from my reverie... Awake, I'll see
how weary you've become. How all along
your story's mine. And how, alone, we belong.

Regarding Grief's Particulars

They never actually tied the "so-called knot,"
he says, so what hold does he have on her remains?
He knows not much, but he'll still try to find out
what's left of her after the autopsy
and all those days she's been at the whim
of the *Medical Center for the Study of the Dead*
or, he says, a place named something close to that.

But it's good, you say, that she gave
her body for the advancement of medicine.
Yes, he supposes that's okay but he needs
to know the state she's in. Right now.
He's waiting for her ashes they promise
they'll Fed-X right here. To this room. With him.
And with the five cats whose names he recites for you.

He says he kind of likes the idea you share
about how you put your mother's ashes
in a pretty box…from Bloomingdale's…
on your mantelpiece. And how you knew one day
she would say that it was time
to be alongside your dad and brother, Mike.
And how late one day you sneaked into the cemetery
with a spade and your mother in the pretty box.
And how you missed her then but how, finally, it felt right.

No hurry, you point out. When she's settled
back here, you'll know just where she wants to be.
Chances are good you say, right here with him.
And the five cats he names like saints.

Although I Am the One Sent to Help

On the sofa you are rounded beneath
your comforter, knees drawn toward
the source of your fever. The room
wavers with your heat. And this

is where I come in, blue around the lips
and bent by the darkness of this mid-
afternoon. Between the hallway's doors,
I bang the snow from my boots, shake

the weather from the wool vaults
of my hat and coat. Even so, I move
toward you like a storm. But if I am
a specter of winter's gloom,

you never let on, and reaching
for my hands, you offer to warm them.

Visiting Nurses, Bridgeport, Connecticut, circa 1985

The phones, black boxes the weight of stones
size for size, measured 10 inches long, 5 inches wide.
She can't say how deep. Only how ponderous hers felt close
to her side. How its shoulder strap unbalanced her stride.

Not one ounce of nonsense, the black boxes were the armor
their job required, riding city project elevators some distance
from earth, their lookout back in their unmarked van, watching
for any deal gone bad. A deadly feud. Phones to beckon

them back. Calls to get them out. And she thought, *You could
die getting back to the van.* Still, they only rode
morning hours when dealers slept and gangs only dreamed
restless dreams of payback. You could, she thought,

die in the elevator where strangers rang to stop
your ride on a floor where you did not plan to stop. You
could die if the boyfriend who'd been out of town stops
back for a place to sleep. Back for more than a bite to eat.

But she and her V.N.A. gang brought coffee those days
they rode with the off-duty cops. They joked and put
their heads together in the back of the jostling van,
foreheads bumping, coffee spilling

over their big-plan chart to get so-and-so out
of his pinch, so sick. So broke. Oh, all the usual stuff
that they could sometimes fix. All the usual stuff that
no one could fix. And they grabbed their phones and got to it.

The Social Worker Takes Note

on Widower K's Relocation

The entrance to Mr. K's room is around the back
of the owner's house. On the open porch,
two tarnished cats set themselves against a sun
stuck at 2 o'clock. Your shadow falls across each one

with no apparent loss of light or warmth. At the yard's
far end, a dog is set in the black cut-out
of his house. And although you wave your hands
and call the dog the dozen dog names you know,

no tail registers your noise. No eye squints
to let you in. Perched on the porch's
uncertain boards, you wait for some sign that you
have come. On a straight-backed chair

the man inside waits too. Even though he knows
the truth, he waits for his wife to trim his hair,
to lift the hair at the nape of his neck, her own hair,
despite its clips, tumbling over his.

Despite so many moves, since his army days
he has never had to pack. He will wait for her.
At least to show him how to fold his underwear
and roll his socks. To choose what would be best

to leave. But she has not come. Although you finally knock
and Mr. K, rising from his straight-backed chair, calls
to the door, to the air it holds back, that he'll be right there,
no dog looks up. No cat. The sun remains at two o'clock.

A Lesson in Listening

Home Visit 7/7/2010

You've just met and sit across
from each other at her kitchen table.
She's out of breath, she says,

and with the slightest bit of work...
with no more than a breath...
the fractures in her spine spread.

This year her garden will have to hang
from the porch rail in pots. As hard
as surrender is, she's hired someone

to mop. No one is needed to straighten up.
She's perfectly neat, she says, and humbled
having to ask for help.

She catches her breath. Admires
your pants. Your beads. Your
pep. Tells you that once, at a fair,

she rode a camel with her son
when he was six. Her daughter
was too little then. To ride.

That's what a mother does. She
rides. Or judges when not
to risk the height of a camel's back.

She tells you she rarely shares
with anyone that her children both
are dead. Not long dead.

That's all she tells. Her kitchen chair
   creaks. Their absence
                         descends.

How She Escapes

for Lisa

She's crossed into a vague geography
where her diagnosis spans the sky
and neither sun nor rain falls
where she sets down one foot

and then the next. Where she must
rest. Where the roof holds nothing
back because nothing rides the air.
She's tired of plucking a bright

word or two from the *blah,*
blah, blah of pain. She can no longer name
the day. Or, named, find
meaning in it.

Her son stays away. She dreams
he falls from the sky, like sun or rain.

Starting Out

So Soon

Sleep, my child, and peace attend thee...
—from the lullaby "All Through the Night"

I was too young to drive when
we rounded a hill I imagined
myself dead and buried in.

What was it about that rise
toward knotty woods that drew me
to its unattended sleep?

I turned to my father at the wheel
to find his profile stilled by the need
to keep his eye on what lay ahead.

And we drove and drove past hill
after hill without a word and I
never asked and he never said.

Grief's Job

For Mike (1942-1979)

Grief's sprawled, you discover, in his folding chair
with, it now appears, no standards to consider.
You'd been certain he'd be flat out bored
with you and your long parade of sorrows.

That he'd have slipped off just anywhere
for a break from the yada-yada of your fervent prayers,
no less from your once-certain notion
that in the morass of loss, you alone were down,

sniffling back tears on the Stop and Shop line, undone
and wondering why neither the unscathed person
before you, nor the one behind, took your hand
to help stem the brim of grief you couldn't contain.

You never saw grief's chair parked hard by every line,
feet outstretched to deck you again. Or anyone. Anytime.

I've Tried to Say This Before

about the taut wire
that bound the four of us
together

in the four-room flat
that held us closer than
was good for us. No where
to go but out. No where

to go when it was too late
to slip away. Too late
in the day. Too late
in the morass of that

and every other day. My father
clinking away with his
jigger, bottle and glass.
My brother, elbowing

his way out, drink in hand.
My mother smoothing out
the dish towel, folding it
exactly over the bar

of our oven door. A perfect
rectangle. Both before
and aft. I, too, folded
in half. Silent and

exact, with only
this to name it.

Children's Hour

For Mike (1942-1979)

We'd determined the most disgusting
and bravest act was touching tongues
and so, with an occurrence as unpredictable as
childhood's trajectory, we'd stick out

our tongues and, despite squeals
and our bodies' lurch, touch the very tip
of each other's tongues, only to run
to any corner far from the other's reach until,

possessed, another hour or another day,
we'd dare again to discover the limits of our
bravery. I cannot say what brought a sister
and kid brother to such squeamish territory. Finally,

it seems, if touching tongues had meaning then,
it's lost to the then young me. To the long-gone him.

In a New York Minute

For Mike (1942-1979)

We were raised in Parkchester,
the Bronx. Potted philodendron
on windowsills. The occasional
patch of fenced grass. In high-rises'

long shadows where we hung out, sparrows
hung out. My kid brother dubbed them
Parkchester Birds...a summing up of our
natural world. Until, kid brother still, behind

a runaway wheel, he quit our grownup world.
Ice, I've heard, will have all but disappeared
from the Arctic Ocean by the summer of 2,040.
Today, on my afternoon swim, I dream

the two of us traversing that expanding reach...
two Bronx kids, by then two Bronx fish.

In the End

For Deedee

       it was this: her legs elephantine
with the flood her heart ignored,
pumping, instead, oxygen to her vigilance.
To her fuss over the pantyhose she'd rolled neat as gifts,

now useless in her bureau's polished tray.
To her fuss over her Bloomingdale's pumps, freshly heeled
for walks uptown, stymied on the closet floor.
She'd never learned to drive, after all.

Where was that heart of hers then, refusing
to pay off those afternoons she'd plowed up the hill,
North Avenue to Main, her heels clicking off the miles,
her stride denying the press of years, the mornings

of sorrows she arranged like prayers and tucked
precisely into her just-so chest of drawers?

Pushing "M" for Main

In our living room my mother
painted one wall raspberry.

Like sherbet, she said. For summer
she laid down rugs of woven straw

and covered our sofa with a throw
strewn with red roses, appliqued and serious.

It was a place to remain, cooled
with window fans and pulled shades,

a place to wait for evening.
For my father's uncertain coming home.

But with what little thought, except
for the elevator's ride to our street's

wavering heat and to my friends,
hands on their hips, waiting for me,

I closed the door on that sweet pretense
and all that my mother intended for us.

Hope's Design

Despite

his daily, jaunty
start,
despite

his toilet,
door shut,
the sink water he runs
to outdo the splash
of his lesser self,
despite

his constant cigarette,
exactly held, smoke up,
his fingers pristine,
despite

his fedora's
precise finish, atop
the smart angles
of his a.m. face
as he heads out

by some mistake

the Prince each morning
we convince ourselves
we can rely upon

comes undone,

barely aloft in his
ash-smudged suit,
his fedora gone
those unsteady nights
he confuses
our hallway closet
for the toilet,
despite its lack
of running water
for cover.

And then another morning
comes around.
                    Yet again.

Choosing the First Among Equals

Who could decide
which one would come first? Look.
Here they are where we started out

in our Bronx, two-bedroom flat where
we wove and interwove ourselves:
She, who dusted the newest dust with the hem

of her skirt on her way to answer the door.
Who, smart as she was, begged for things
to change. I heard her begging from every room.

And he who poured the drinks and peered
through the always-smoke in which he dwelled,
half-disappeared in some lost dream. Or at least

some dream I assigned to him. And the boy who darted
with no tale to tell except what could be read into
his *Vroom, vroom!* above his Dinky Toys.

(From his collection, I've arranged a car,
a plane, a truck. A memorial
of sorts. A memorial banged up.)

It went on and on this way until our home
seemed, if not grand or comforting,
at least a predictable place...

a dream to dwell, not unlike
the moment you light a cigarette, your breath
as deep as the breath of sleep, the smoke sweet,

meandering from room-to-room where neither
dust nor drinks nor the blur of a darting boy
tells me which one to remember first.

Which of them, despite what I begin to see
I haven't accounted for, would best be put
before the rest.

Linen takes the hottest iron,

                              power too,
my full weight pressed onto the iron's weight.
The bond we make to diminish linen's resistance.
In the time it takes to tame my jacket's seams, time rewinds

to that afternoon my brother, home from his day at school,
came across our mother's struggle bent over the board
she'd squeaked open in our apartment kitchen,
her iron stomping damp, indiscernible heaps beneath

its stainless heat and, with a pivot
toward the stove's spotless top, dropping item
after steaming now geometric item
upon the pristine range's out of sight lit pilot light.

With dinner hours hence, he tossed off his bag
of books, cajoling her to elucidate just what *was*
that strange instrument she was wielding there.
A joke delighting her despite its ironic implication

that she wasn't well acquainted
                    with all it takes to press
                                        life into subjugation.

My Mother Thought to Watch Out for Me

Decades ago, with her hands on her hips,
her words arrived quietly. Between her teeth,

love swallowed hard, when time and again
she'd turn on her heel to advise me,

her apologetic child, not to apologize
when apology had nothing to do with it. *You,*

dear girl, did nothing untoward. That voice
that would admonish me...

sidewalk, supermarket, library,
church aisle, bus stop...not to be

a goddamn fool. Not to be stuck
in sentiment. In deference. Today her scold

arrives to scorn my fussy polishing.
So what that silver tray had once been

in her provenance? So what, I'd taxed it
with stacks of exhausted flower pots?

It's only silver plate, she'd say. Stop
fussing over it. It's not worth a thing...

Not money.
Not memories.

And Then

The Gathering

of the Terhorsts, O'Briens, and Manders

On the deck, we lounge
in a dalliance of torsos and limbs.
Acorns drop their autumnal noise.
Here. Here. Then there.

Julian swept the deck
early in the day with his grandmother's broom
and now it seems it was never swept
and he must sweep again.

Gage names songs he's learned
in music school and sings bits
and phrases from *Yesterday*.
We all turn to listen and join in

here and there.
Emma moves her camera away
from our today to play a loop
of Julian jumping into the pool.

She plays and he jumps in, jumps in, jumps in.
The afternoon sun drops below the hills.
Shadows lengthen over us and on
to the waiting woods.

It took lifetimes to bring us here
from everywhere.

Letter from a Day at the Beach Bereft, July 9th

For Peter, Paul's loving twin

Dear Uncle Paul,

You're not missing much here today,
the summer sun's insistence given
what-for by an offshore breeze and
a haze that blurs all of us to a barely
manageable brilliance.

Not to say you were one to pontificate—
but I can hear your take on this light
and this air, your take on the water
from the vantage of your director's chair.
With one eye shut, you'd measure

the spot a swimmer could skirt the rocks, there,
just down the beach from the volleyball net. And, of course,
your warning that the water's surface is just
warm enough to trick you into its icy deep.
That, you'd say, *is just the nature of existence.*

Oh, OK then, and good enough!
Without you to sum it all up, today is not
that much, your broad expanse
in this universe shifted, your chair
folded and stacked behind the house...

Surrender Is at Least as Sweet

For John

It's true you never did toss your socks and shoes
onto the sand, despite my wish…my certainty…
you'd love what I love about the sea, about
its diminishment at your feet. The spike
of sand your heels kick up along that line
the elements exchange their temporary vows.
Their taking leave. Their starts. Their stops.
But finally, I've learned to love,

your lack. The sigh I know you're sighing
of relief. And I, left alone to witness sand
and sea, am free to enter into their constant
ceremony with no need for your words of praise.
No need to tolerate your vague complaints
mumbled just ahead…or just in back of me.

The Earth

In memory of Elliot Hertz 5/5/42-4/7/20

on its axis spun a bazillion years without one word and, without
one thought about the way the marsh grass lies flat beneath wind's
winter knife. Well, I guess, not quite. Wind's knife, of course, does
all the work. But by the time our minds work it out, spring's pushed
up its first naïve, green darts. In a Nassau hospital,

our *machatunim* barely breathes. He's said he'll stay there for the
oxygen to which they've hooked him up. "Right here," he says,
"for heaven's sake." His wife, his girls, all kept afar, fumble through
their divided days. We write flowered notes or sorry jokes to pass
along by mail. Still, before any thoughts arrived on earth, before
the words

to spell them out, the world would have marked his fragile state with
nothing but a glance. No. Not even that. No eyes to differentiate his
eyes, half closed. No eyes to weep. No words to note our sorrow's
brevity, our need to wrap it up, to tuck it all away until another,
settled day. That day we look up from the morning news and think

about those too few times we'd met. How his eyes would close with
a knowing laugh when he joked about life's ironies. And now, how
we barely have the words for that.

Taking Care of Birds and Other Small Creatures

Newtown, Sandy Hook, Connecticut, December 14, 2012
"The grief will not end. Yet the healing must begin."
—Associated Press

The bird feeders have been empty for over
three weeks. Last evening, sparrows,
brown and forlorn as the broken leaves
scattered across our lawn, hovered
above the feeders and poked the darkening air,
only to fly far from the ice-shorn marsh
behind our house.

Feeding the birds is my job at this house
of ours, which is one story and just right
for the two of us now, without the boys
whose tossed-off sneakers had rerouted the way
through our old rambling Cape, whose voices
could jar even those beyond noise. Who wrestled
the desks and chairs along with themselves
onto our hardwood floors, until one, then the next,
tall as men and wise, packed up
their childhood, paused for a hug and left
that big house of ours stone-still.

Now, from our low perch here, we glimpse them
now and then, their own fledglings
not far behind, sneakers in hallways...
piles and piles of them...
jostling for space, poised for flying.

This afternoon my husband says
before I can say what is always mine to say,
Let's fill the bird feeders today.
Without more being said

we haul on our hats and coats,
click the door closed on the unfolding news
of the first graders, sneakers snug
on their now-stilled feet,
and head to the feeders aloft
                on the winter-bright air.

The Buddhists Say

after Dutiyachiggaḷayuga Sutta

For Michael Sean

if the earth, top-to-bottom, were endless sea,
and if but one blind turtle, swam therein,
and if that turtle came up for air
but once every 1,000 years...and if but one

lifesaving ring tossed wave-to-wave along
that endless sea...odds of that turtle popping in-
to that preserver's bobbing hospitality were
approximately the same as the serendipity of

your arriving, head-to-toe, a human being. Now,
imagine adding this to a human's happenstance:
a Keurig on the granite counter; an A.C. in the window;
a patio behind your house facing the marsh, where,

on occasion, you are mindlessly gazing
                    when your son paddles by, waving.

Grappling

A perfect drying day, sheets full sail in the sun
the wind endeavors to shade with strident,
indecisive clouds, the last sheet, no sooner
pinned than the first, dry and blank white,

lifts above your line, beckoning you to
batten it down, along with its attendant
gusts and light, into the steady wicker
at your feet, and you lift and haul the basket

informed by all that's captured in the careless
folds of tackled flat and contoured sheets,
the blousy hills of shams, until,
at your back door, you stall before taking

the step you must take into your house's past
and all that's next. Into its more or less.

And So

Revisiting a Youthful Conversation on Love's Meaning

after Li-Young Lee's exploration of words' meanings

You remarked on its *dangerousness*.
No?   Then it was death
you named,
a grave *passion* akin
to *love*.   Nonsense,
you protest.   Well, go back
to the night
we walked along Riverside Drive,
with barely a word.   Block
after block, the measuring sticks
of the river's dark rush, its lighted banks,
our faint hold on what we knew of life.

As good as dead you said.   I had known
little enough about death until then: a school friend,
22, stationed in Bermuda (say *Heaven*)
killed on a routine sortie, *flying*.
And would he have refused to write his
love so high above his just-taken bride
had he dreamed he'd abandon her
as she turned in her sleep.

She mistook
love for *promise*.

Oh, perhaps that night by
the river it was I who said *dangerous*.   It was the first
I knew of it.

Or of *fate* (say *God*), one had to conclude

is (choose) indifferent or *dangerous*:
a doubtful   lesson

                        on how *love* rules.

Cold in the Country, Notwithstanding

What's missing now is the city bus stop
mid-February when the bus doesn't come and
you're sure your icy end is ascending from
your steaming boots, the escaping
groans of the rest, huddled collar-to-collar,
your fates certain.

What's missing now is each of you pounding
your quilted sleeves, glaring down the distance
of the slushy avenue, as if glares will materialize
the bus meant to deliver you exactly to the spot
for which you'll so smartly alert the driver.

What's missing now is the #M101 that you and your
single-minded kith finally succeed in conjuring
from its distant tease to its door panting open
before your collective misery.

What's missing now is its gleaming flight
of stairs inviting you to ENTER HERE.

What's missing now is the steam your breath
bequeaths the driver as you drop your token
down her endless repository of fares. Your
thank you prayers for the behemoth's rush
of heat. For its one vacant plastic bucket seat.

What's missing now is the steamy window you rub
with a thawing sleeve to watch for the next huddled band
of commuters craning for a sighting of your bus and which,
once onboard, you'll thank for its collective breath. Its heat.
Its muttered prayer. Or, at least, the muttered prayer
you're sure you heard.

What's missing now
is the street's indifference,
the blighted snow, the *Bus Stop*.
You. The bus. The rest, warming
each-to-each, until your reluctant exit
at 3rd and 96th.

Reverie

"Southern border sees largest number of migrants" —ABC News

The dock bobbing on the cove this breezy sun-in, sun-out day,
is tethered to a ramp edging up the hill to the thousand
steps heading to a house, higher still…so high it's lost in
woods and clouds snagged in the tree's canopy. But nobody

descends. Nobody sails down the stairs to land upon
the undulating invitation to this blue perfection. And with
no one to shake a finger at your audacity, you spy a family
emerging from the terror they've just fled. Their clamber

over the wall. Their surprise to discover a path to the thousand
steps to the bobbing dock…its invitation to swim awhile. To
            lounge
until sandwiches are served. Ice cream. Coffee, just percolated.
Until, on the dock's slatted bench, *The Book of Magic*,

nudged open by a breeze, reveals the dream
that landed them right there. And the hour they will have to leave.

This fly,

trapped by the seal
of my window's twin glass,
grand view through its inedible
sandwich,

is frantic to discover the secret
of the maze she sees etched
by sun and dust!
Wide-eyed, she would dive

against either paradise, but all she does
is buzz and flutter toward one side
and then the other. My front yard
droops with summer.

On the corner of my mirror
I have propped a rose.
She preens for both but will wither
in her airless zone,

her wings no room to fly,
while I before my mirror
comb my hair
and hum...she and I.

Without a Word

after Judy Perry's painting of the Labrador retriever, Sally

Sally, like all household gods, chooses
not to talk. She keeps her compassion
and wisdom to herself, except

for the occasional telltale sign, like
her look, so pensive, you glimpse
the all-knowing god she is. She's seen you

pace the floor, heard the cascade
of your tears, read the too-long silence
of an abandoned argument. Heard

the back door slam. Her remedy
is in her majesty. She looks up
from where she sits and offers you

the touchstone of her crown
and lifted, silken ears. And when
your distracted glance enters

her unflinching gaze, she holds
your distress in her wordless
amazing grace.

For the Girl Who'd Make Poems of Whales

Poetry Night at the Open Mic

She waltzes her whale like
a crinoline the night before
the dance, around the room,

One, two, three,
one, two, three,
held to her waist,

his baleen at her cheek…
he will take a small nip
from her neck only later,

her hair in streams
from his mouth
like vapor.   For now

he will oblige her
and dance, oil smoldering
under his white expanse,

with only sweet hints
of his unctuousness.

Grief: A Tip or Two on How to Handle It

It's the unpredictable size of grief that gives you the biggest headache, not to say heartache. Just when you think you've got the hang of it, when you think you know how to file it away, to say "There.

That takes care of it," a new grief whose tiny shape and suddenness has been, up until that moment you spy it outside your window on just the right/wrong day, without consequence, knocks you off stride, you have

no remedy except to straighten your spine, turn on your heel. Make a cup of tea. Not that you don't care about the woman walking now without the toddler who tagged along all spring. Not even that you know his toddler fate. He may,

after all, just be too grown now to tag along. He may, after all, not be dead or missing. Still, this mother, alone on your summer street, changes how you see the leafed-out trees. How you perceive the curve of the street disappearing east.

So, sip your tea. Write this poem. Print it with margins neither too narrow nor deep. Punch holes in it. File it in the binder you label *Grief*. See the way the window sees.

Joy and How to End It

Take the half-moon that appeared exactly in the top
left grid of your 6-over-4 double hung window
onto the October night. Something, you thought,
turning back to your work, like a Sharpie's bright stroke,

a highlight you might discover on a calendar
you hadn't referenced in a while, and you
wonder what on earth it signifies. Whether
to mark the anniversary of some

momentous date like Hannah's birth.
Or to mark the day you had to call
your friend next door before she moved
from your world to a state too far for tea and toast.

A date you'd once thought you'd never
neglect. Or someone's death, years before,
that you'd let slip by. But before all that,
in the moment before your mind

yanks you from the jolt of the moon's perfect
half, dropped from the sky's impossible
height into the precise niche
of your dreamy sight, you

are moon and windowpane and day and night
and sky and room, your hands poised above
your keyboard with nothing,
nothing on your mind.

Not that Far

She had asked if they couldn't exit I-95
to stop at the Bay whose estuaries floated in
and out of sight. But he had said *No*.
It was getting too late, especially on such

a long ride up the coast. Later, when from
their indoor pool's westward window she saw beyond
the trees what seemed, through the Jacuzzi steam,
a blazing sunset that was, she realized

actually the corrugated roof
of Houlihan's Brewery, she made up her mind
that it was brilliant enough and all right. Now,
swimming the pool's length, she decides

her legs fluttering the water still look
sturdy. Her arms, still strong, flinging back.

A Lesson in Alternative Medicine

With thanks to Greg

"Imagine," he says, holding his right hand
just above his forehead, his left hand
level with the crook of his elbow,
"a string, or, better yet, a ribbon"

and I think, enough pink grosgrain
to secure a small, perfect gift, and he says,
"Imagine your spine as you tug
your right hand up a notch, again

and then again until you've reclaimed
your unbowed back," and I think of my pain
as a present waiting to be freed from its wrap:
a crow or a rabbit or an unsprung bud

lifting its head to the surprise of the sun,
whether to fly. To hop. To blossom.

Summer's Prosody

Poems arrive on the breeze fluttering a field's wildflowers,
words riding the petals' fair colors and dropping them
onto the poet's lined journal before she knows
what her fingers know about all the breeze delivers...
gayety or impermanence or the season's promise.

And although she does not name more than she sees,
mysteries reside inside her words, latent and haunting,
until one day, coming across her poem, you too see the field,
the flowers flying. And, transported by all the poet says,
and all not said, the breeze arrives, nonetheless.

By Happenstance: A Tale

Her name is Princess,
his, Jose. Her hair, painted
aubergine, traverses her face
with every breeze. When I offer
to take the selfie they're trying to take,
we chat a bit, as is anybody's way.

When I warn
that their faces will be lost
in the shadow of the water's glare,
Jose says he doesn't care...they need to pose there
before the sea, their likely disappearance
the price they'll pay. Every year now,

Jose says, they journey to Westerly,
despite how sad he gets as they pass
the house of his friend's mother,
now deceased. He'd helped his friend
take care of her. He loved her and is sad
every time. Yes, every time. But grateful, too, he says...

They rode their motorcycle here,
I learn, as I contemplate *Reverse*
in my Subaru and cocktails ahead,
the rough blare of their engine heats
the lot's black top. Roughs up
everyone's signed-off ears.

Their music, blasting confident,
        rouses the evening's drowsy heat.
                Lifts gulls' wings.

All late winter, early spring,

I stormed the beach, breath steaming
curses against the cold,
pretending myself warm, damning
the useless sun. Today the sun
brought Jose and Princess,
my erstwhile useless curses undone.

And as the sun bows out to eventide,
Jose and Princess, helmets strapped
and certain for the Interstate, roar away
in opposition to the lot's arrowed path,
repainted last season ... faint now but,
nonetheless, still able to convey the safe way.

His friend's mother's house,
empty still, awaits their passing by.
He'll nod to her then, even as they fly away,
Princess's escaping hair
                        banner of love's constancy.

Losing Sight

A clipboard, a *Habitat for Humanity*'s
Jot-a-Note, a retractable pen, offer
themselves to compensate for her

Samsung Galaxy with its perfect eye
that must be sitting on her sideboard where it
hid itself from her on her way out the door.

Now, parked at the beach's edge,
she stares past the mirrored ridge
of sunlight stretched east-to-west

along the horizon's smart mark,
past the gull that thrusts itself sea-
to-sky, only to hover cloud-to-cloud,

before it deigns to swoop to land
on the stolid rock that intrudes itself
between asphalt lot/ridged sand/

ruffled sea. Tucking one leg up,
the gull stares past her Subaru, past
the phone's eye that, left behind,

dulls the gull and sea and sky and leaves
only her, with her last breath before
she backs out, bereft. Lost, the gull,

shadow-to-light, weaving the wind's
warp and woof. Lost, the gull's untamed
shuttle. Lost, its momentary stop.

Lull

after Arthur Heming's The Whiskey Smuggler

Signs of the wind's brash work
remain long after
the jagged air has collapsed
to the wintry earth and lies still,

so still, you can't believe the wind
ever ruled the terrain with such
brouhaha, until you are halted
by its snow-cast aftermath: wild crests,

held fast beneath night's first stars
and day's last shock of light,
where two riders, one a ranger, one
the ranger's bound thief, stall in equipoise.

For now, inside the trees' white trance,
neither man is pressed by the encroaching storm
to gallop fast ahead, all the while listening
for the wind's final howl

to hunker down, to breathe his last
precious heat into the chapel
of his cupped hands,
sun and campfire snuffed dark,

the wind, loosed from heaven
once again, undoing what had been
its own measured
and perfect artistry.

You Question the Recommendation

He opined the best sleep is dreamless sleep.
You wonder, then, how you'd have come upon
the unnamed doctor who unlocked your spine, disk
by disk. Or how you'd have arrived unannounced

at your son's loft to say what you said regarding
the woman about whom he's uncertain.
Or how, without the cold sweat you awakened in,
you'd have known you just missed

the earth-bound plane ablaze in the terminal window.
Or how you'd have finally marked the shadow the cathedral
cast across your doomed family, the sun plummeting
night after night from its heaven. Or how, with all

you've learned asleep, you'd get by without the wisdom
you somehow own but can't quite put your finger on.

Knowing Almost Everything

I'll tell you exactly what I think,
as if I know something in advance
about how the day opens through
a chink in the blind, how it delivers

sadness without a reminder of all
you've learned about how a morning walk
around your neighborhood helps make sense
of things, say, about who's fine and who's

up against it, just by the way a lawn swoops
up to a screen door with, behind it, a red door
ajar to the morning's breeze and early light.
Or how a car, warming up on a driveway,

edges into reverse onto a road that leads,
with just so many lefts and rights, to I-95.
Or how a phone ringing in someone's house
cocks your head toward the silence that rests

between hope and fear. And you are reminded
it's all the same, and for everyone. And there,
on the spot, confidence buoys your step.
If only back to where you started out.

Notes

About the Cover for The Scatter and the Gap
In 2009, Judy Perry, recovering at home from the injuries sustained in a life-threatening automobile accident, was facing challenges to her ability to return to her career as a well-known and respected portrait artist.

To her dismay, she discovered she could barely recall how to hold a paintbrush! What were the chances she'd be able to return to the art that sustained and delighted her and those who loved her work?

And then a fellow-artist, Deborah Quinn-Munson, came to visit. "Well," her friend said, "let's start somewhere!" and together they tore up an old canvas of Judy's and created the collage, *All in Pieces*, that you see on the cover of this book. "The Scatter and the Gap" is the title poem written in response to Judy's work, as well as the title of this entire collection.

Happily, Judy has been able to return to the high level of artistic skill she enjoyed prior to her accident. She can be reached at her website: judyperryart.com.

And Almost Home: This poem is in response to a 16-year-old's accidental death. He was fatally struck by a falling tree during a windstorm in Surrey.

Disconnected: In an interview with Terry Gross on the program Fresh Air, Craig Haney recalled a prisoner in Massachusetts who described disassembling his television set and eating the contents. His medical records confirmed this.

Higgs Boson Leads the Way Back to Empty Space and All That It Contains: Sheldon Lee Glashow, who along with Steven Weinberg and Adbur Salam, won a Nobel Prize in Physics, once referred to the Higgs field as the "toilet" of modern physics, because that's where the ugly details that allow the marvelous beauty of the physical world are hidden.

About the Author

Patricia Horn O'Brien is a graduate of Columbia School of Social Work and has worked and volunteered as a social worker throughout her adult life. She's a member of the Guilford Poets Guild and co-founded the poetry group, Connecticut River Poets. She's helped in the establishment of Prison Hospice in three Connecticut prisons and facilitated poetry workshops with fellow poets at York Correctional Institution. She initiated the ongoing program, *Paintings and Poetry*, at Florence Griswold Museum which includes poets from Connecticut River Poets, GPG, and creative writing students from Old Saybrook High School. Pat's been published in several periodicals and anthologies, including *Connecticut Review*, *Embers*, *Pulp Smith*, *Poet Lore*, *Caduceus*, *Red Fox Review*, *Freshwater*, *Connecticut River Review*, *Laureates of Connecticut*, *Guilford Poets Anthology* and most recently, in the anthology *Waking up to the Earth*.

Her first poetry collection, *When Less Than Perfect is Enough*, published by Antrim House Books, is in its second printing. She and her son Richard Manders co-wrote and published their memoir about their adoption story, *The Laughing Rabbit: A Mother, a Son and the Ties that Bind*, in 2018. Pat is Poet Laureate of Old Saybrook, Connecticut.

Acknowledgments

Some of the poems in this collection have also appeared in *Poet Lore, Pulp Smith, Connecticut River Review, Embers, Bean Feast, Fresh Water, Caduceus, Laureates of Connecticut, Waking Up to the Earth, Where the River Bends*, the *Old Saybrook Historical Society*, and *Poetry and Art Along the Connecticut River.*

I would like to thank my supportive, funny, and patient mate, John, and my immediate and extended family, my friends in and out of poetry circles, and, most especially, share my gratitude to fellow poets in Guilford Poets Guild and in Connecticut River Poets, who have cheered on my poetry pursuits with good nature, insight and gentle nudging. Thanks also to those mentors and teachers who have enhanced my world and my appreciation of literature and poetry, including Dick Allen, Edwina Trentham, Maggie Nelson, and Don Barkin, who gave me the courage and the tools to keep at it. I'm thankful, too, to the Town of Old Saybrook for choosing me to be the town's Poet Laureate.

Special thanks to Mary Guitar, who held my hand through much of the groundwork gathering the poems, cleaning them up, and presenting them in their best light for this publication. Thanks also to Ginny Connors, who agreed to publish my work and who helped present it with her experienced eye and invaluable recommendations.

And, finally, I thank Margaret Gibson, Gordy Whiteman, and Nan Meneely for their willingness to plow through this manuscript and to say what they said.

For over 30 years, I have been a practicing Buddhist. I've been learning, among its many valuable teachings, these vital principles: *Welcome everything. Push nothing away. Don't be attached to an outcome. Be open to all possibilities.*

Lightning Source UK Ltd.
Milton Keynes UK
UKHW021650110123
415158UK00011B/111